The Dragon Story

Elise Farrell

Presentation by *BookLeaf Publishing*

Web: www.bookleafpub.com

E-mail: info@bookleafpub.com

ISBN: 9789395969734

First edition 2022

DEDICATION

To Grandpa

I always said my first published piece would be for you.

Love,

Your Almost-Perfect Granddaughter

ACKNOWLEDGEMENT

Of course, I must begin by acknowledging my parents. Their love for literature and stories has inspired me in more ways than they could ever know and their love for their children has taught me how to pursue a life of virtue. I must also thank my siblings for the countless times they sat and listened to my many plot ideas and random stories.

Thank you to my husband, who strives to live out our marital vows every day all the while challenging me to grow in virtue.

PREFACE

I am a lover of poetry but have never claimed to be a poet…and now my first published work is a set of poems. When it comes to writing poetically, I have a storyteller approach. So for this project, it was all the more fitting to write a children's story based on my childhood.

My parent's goal was a simple one; to teach their children to pursue truth, to search for love, to create beauty, and to live in virtue. They did this through their gift of storytelling. The Dragon Story was a simple tale created by my father as a means to entertain five children as they waited for their mother who ran into the grocery store for 'just' a gallon of milk. Simple, and yet effective. This story, along with the stories read and told by my mother, taught me and my siblings to be courageous and compassionate and to have integrity and faith.

Parking Lot

The green minivan was parked
By the one shady tree.
The door propped open,
A tired Papa at the wheel,
Five children squirming,
Fighting for space,
Amongst all the luggage.

"Papa je suis fatigué."
"Je suis faim."
"Non, j'ai faim."
"Thats what I said!"
"No it's not!"

The older children bickered,
The baby began to cry.

"Have I ever told you the story of the prince and
the pirates?"

Child eyes widened with wonder.
Tears were restrained to a sniffle.
They crept forward to the edge of their seats.
"Non, papa."
They all said.

Papa smiled.
He sat up, straight in his seat
At the front of the vehicle
And looked back lovingly at his children
Through the review mirror.

"Alors, écoute bien. Tu êcoute?"
"Oui, papa!"
He nodded his head
And for a moment was silent
Before the great tale began.

Little did the children know,
The adventure that awaited them.

"Il était une fois..."

Il Était Une Fois

Once upon a time,
As all great tales began,
A young man,
A handsome man,
A man of strength and courage,
Stumbled into a great kingdom.

He dared request
An audience with the king.

The king was a wise man;
Noble beyond riches.
He heard of the stranger
And invited him to his banquet.

That evening the stranger,
A kingdomless prince,
Dined in great hall.
The king saw in his guest
A leader
A ruler.

But the festivities of the night
Came to a halt
With the sound of the horn.
The horn whose bellow
Could be felt through the bone.
A deep horn
A war horn.

Magical Mother

Mother returned to the minivan
With a gallon of milk
And bags of groceries.
Brother hopped out
To help her load.

Mothers are quite magical, you know.
The food would become dinner,
Just as their new house
Would become a home.

"And then what papa?"

"Ah oui, les pirates."

Les Pirates

They came in the night,
The men of the sea,
To pillage hallow riches,
And rage death and pain.

The screams of the people
Echoed in the night,
To be heard for centuries to come.

Homes destroyed,
Innocents lost.

Amidst the chaos,
The dark,
Beauty was found.
A small flicker of flame,
The prince's pursuit.

School Day

The young girl followed
The flying trees.
Sometimes she could see a monkey,
Or the man of the jungle,
Swinging through the air
Attempting to keep her pace.

Her sad sighs collected
As fogs on the window.
Her cheek pressed against
The palm of her hand.

"Papa! Tell, us the dragon story!"

The once invisible sounds
Of her sister's chatter
Became reality.
She perked up,
Adjusting her seatbelt.

Maybe being a kingdomless prince,
Felt like sitting alone in a cafeteria.
Maybe knowing a dragon was coming,
Was liking knowing what lurked
Around the corner
Of the bathroom hallway.

"Le prince a trouvé sa princesse."

La Princesse

Her hair was like a golden waterfall.
It rippled and shone in the sun.
Her eyes were blue like the morning sky
Or like a robins egg.
But even more beautiful than her physique
Was the heart that lay beneath.

Amidst the terror
She floated.
The gates of the courtyards
Opened wide.
Shelter to the homeless,
Food to the hungry,
Comfort to the afflicted.

However, beauty draws the eye of many.
Some pursue it with love,
While others search for it in vain.
She was the pirates' ultimate prize

The prince saw the gaze of the pirate king
Rest upon the princess sweet.

The malicious marauder sneered,
Slaughtering his way to his prize.

The prince battled his way forward,
Vanquishing many of the raiding crew.
His mission to protect.

Yet the battle was done
As swiftly as it had begun.
The valiant efforts of the king's men,
Led by prince,
Saved many people.

However, as they watched the ships sail away,
Their beauty forced aboard,
The people mourned,
The princess lost,
And the kingdom was thrust into darkness.

Work Day

The familiar sound
Of the vehicle on the dirt driveway
Brought joy and laughter
Within the small, white mountain house.

The rooms echoed with a chorus of
"Father is home!"
Followed by squeals
And the pittar patter of small feet.

The older sister dried the last dish,
Before taking the hand of the youngest,
And ambling to the door.
The younger children jumped
With outstrethed hands
As papa walked into their home.

He wore a smile
But the older sister could see
Lines of exhaustion
And the dimmed light of his eyes.

She sat in the living room
A game on the floor
With her younger sisters
And her younger brother
She moved her piece when prompted
But her mind was on the closed bedroom door

And the hushed voices behind.

Later that evening,
All the children climbed onto one bed
As they did every night.
Mother walked in with a smile,
A sad smile.

She joined them on the bed,
Book in hand.
When finally the older sister
Had the courage to ask.
"What are we going to do, maman?"

Maman smiled.
"We are going to pray."

The next morning,
A weekday morning,
Older sister watched
As mother hung the laundry outside
She turned to her father who sat with his coffee,
"Papa, tell us the dragon story."
"Yes! Where did the pirates take the princess?"
The rest of the children gathered around.
Father nodded.

"Dacour. Les moi voir… le marais."

Le Marais

All mourned the loss of the princess;
Yet some chose to hope.

The prince,
Determined,
Zealous,
Rallied the kings men;
And with the ruler's blessing
Set sail after the pirates.

Their pursuit led them
To the depths of a swamp;
A jungle of darkness,
Of danger,
Spectral.

Now the king's fleet
Was mighty,
Was swift.
Soon flashes of enemy flags
Could be seen through the vines,
Through trees
Through thicket.

Brick Building

The children squirmed,
Sitting on the grass,
Besides a brick building.

They had been here before,
This same tree,
These same bricks.

This day they had eaten their fill
Of their picnic lunch;
And they eyed the reflective
Tinted doors,
Restless.

Finally, the doors opened.
Out came papa
His hand to the back of his neck,
Sighing.

The children scrambled
With squeals of delight.
The littlests ran
Arms open wide.

"C'est presque fini?"
A daughter asked.

"Oui, ma cherie.
Maman has a few more papers to sign
Pour ton papa."

He led them to the car
Where they all climbed inside.
Then he made his way to the wheel,
Turned on the ignition.

He turned around with a smile.
"Alors, the prince went after the pirates."
He began.

The children began to wiggle,
Full of anticipation,
The suspense.

"But the pirates and the prince did not know…
About le serpent."

Le Serpent

Deep dark depths
Conceal that
Which beg to remain
Hidden,
In wait,
Hunting for prey.

For evils exist
That seek to kill
All that is fair
All that is beautiful
All that is true
All that is good.

Yet for every evil
Fights a good
For every peril
Lives courage.

The pirates
Sounded the alarm
When they caught the first glimpse
Of the king's mighty fleet.

The prince heard their signal.
He rallied the soldiers
To prepare for battle;
Le battaile du Marais.

Arrows flew through the air;
King arrows,
Pirate arrows.
Canyon shots were fired;
Marauder canyons,
Royal canyons.

Men lined the decks;
Swords in hand,
Cutless' swinging
Yet no one would have
The chance to cross.
No one would leave their ship.

The water erupted,
Waves thrown to the air.
The ships rocked
Side to side,
Nearly colliding.

Le serpent du marais.

It began to twist
Its roped scales around
The raider ship.

The valiant prince
Climbed to the top.
From the crow's nest he swung.

Spurred by his bravery
King's men followed suit.
Both pirate and soldier
Fighting the monster.

The prince searched for the princess,
But all in vain,
For the pirate king,
In a wicked act,
Had taken her aboard
His spare vessel
And left his sinking
Ship behind.

His men enraged
Ceased to fight
The prince's men.
All forces were now
Fixed on the serpent.

Every blade,
Every arrow,
Was driven into its side.
Until it reared its mighty head,
Writhing with wrath.

The prince once more
Took to the air
Swinging high
With might,
Sinking steel
Into the serpent's
Cavernous jaw.

New House

The woods were a realm of their own,
Endless.
The dirt road climbed
Higher up the mountain
Until finally
They came around the bend.

Their piece of paradise;
Away from the noise,
The chatter,
The piercing eyes,
With judgemental glares.

The last of the boxes
Were unloaded;
Another stone
For the parlor fort.
Small heads popping up
From behind its tall walls.

A single tear
On older sister's face,
As she remembered their old home;
Their room,
Their knight,
Their dragon.

Father entered.
He inspected the fort
And gave an approving nod.

"This makes me think of a story…"

Squeals of delight
Erupted from amidst
The jungle of boxes
And little bodies crawled
Through the cardboard tunnels

"The dragon story papa!"

They gathered around
As father sat
On his plastic wrapped
Green chair.

"Le prince chased the pirate king
Until he found the black ship
Anchored at the beach
Of l'île."

L'Île

It was a mountainous island;
Rocky ridged,
Willow wooded,
Coastal cliffed.

Uninhabitated;
Silent but for the wind
That crashed against the bluffs,
Like the waves of the ocean upon the shore.

The prince looked through his telescope.
He scanned the ship,
He searched the shore.
Was this to be a battle of land?
Or was this to be a battle of sea?

Night Shift

The older sister entered the home;
Her feet were blistered,
Her muscles on fire,
Uniform in disarray.

The first of the younger children
Had just descended the stairs.
Rubbing her eyes
She poured a cup
Of café au lait;
One for herself
And one for the older sister.

"Mother went to work this morning.
Father is off today."

It had been a lifetime
Since the family shared
A morning meal.

The older sister sipped her drink,
Enveloped in comfort
Ready for sleep.

Then a pitter patter of feet
Rushed down into the kitchen.
Youngest sister,
Dawned in her nightgown.

"Father said he would tell us the dragon story
If we bring him coffee!"

Older sister had grown too much
For such stories.
She had aged out of fairy tales
And was too weary
To stay up another moment.

"Go on ahead. I will bring his coffee
As I make my way to bed."

It took every strength
Older sister had
To pull herself
Up the steps,
Steaming mug in hand.

She entered her parent's bedroom
Greeted by love
Emersed in laughter
Perhaps, she could sit and listen
Just for a moment.

Perhaps,
One does not age out of fairytales
But rather they age into them.

"The pirates awaited the prince
And his men.
They stood as a battalion
Upon the shore.
The prince called to his soldiers;
Prepare…
C'est l'heure de la bataille."

La Battaille

Proud, patient pirates
Waited on the shore
Sneering, snivling snides
Hands tight upon
The hilts of their cutlass'.

Proud, protector prince
Searched for the princess.
Strong, steadfast soldiers
Braced themselves for battle.

There she stood,
A rose against the treeline,
Bound and gagged,
Eyes blazing with courage.

The kingsmen cautiously
Approached the island beach;
Never losing sight
Of the evil seamen.

But the mauraders mission
Was to instill fear.
They allowed the prince
And his soldiers
To step foot on dry soil.

They were hungry for blood;
But blood shed in terror
Felt far more gratifying
Then blood of mere opportunity.

There was a moment
Where all was still;
Men in armor,
Men in sea cloth.
All want what is beautiful
But not not all want to love,
To protect,
To serve.

Then with a war cry,
Chilling to the bone,
Yearning for their princess,
The kingsmen,
Led by the prince,
Charged forward,
And the battle began.

Saturday Pancakes

The older sister
Wanted nothing more
Then to slam her head
On the rustic dining table.
She hated writing.
She hated words.

"No you don't."
Mother would remind.
"You simply hate organizing."
Then a few notecards,
And color coded notes later,
An essay magically appeared.

And then as if by reward,
A whimsical scent,
Mouthwatering,
Drifted through the air.

Saturday morning pancakes;
Or better yet,
A rare weekend morning
Where Papa home.

A rush of feet descended the stairs;
Wrinkled nightwear,
Rubbing eyes,
Papa's accented laugh.

"Clear the table!"
He proclaimed.

A pitcher of juice
Café au lait
Sticky maple syrup
Essay pushed aside.

The clink of silverware to plates.
Smiles and chuckles,
Satisfied appetites.

"Papa, who won the battle?
What happened next?"

Papa sipped his coffee,
A mischievous smile,
"Hm… did I forget to mention
Le dragon?"

Le Dragon

The battle raged on.
The once serene island
Now drenched in chaos;
But little did they know
Of the darkness the island hid.

The ground began to ruthlessly rumble.
The mountains began to quake.
Men both soldier and pirate
Were thrown to their knees.

A mighty roar,
Like that of a thousand thunders,
Rang out across the island.

Then it appeared.

A beast erupted from the mountain's peak;
Enraged, egregious, evil,
With wings that veiled the sun,
Scales as strong as kingly armor,
And claws like tree trunks
Sharp as steel.

In one fell swoop
He descended upon the chaos.
A claw enclosed itself around the princess
And he lifted her into the air
Disappearing at the mountain's peak.

River Side

She was living life
As if of a dream
A scene from a storybook
Yet the story they are in
Is never recognized
Until the book is closed.

A small apartment
Over a french café,
Beside a river,
Across which sat
A vibrant greenhouse.
Blooms and buds
Every shape
Every color.

The older sister
Sat on the balcony;
Piles of texts
Papers and pens,
Inhaling the northern
Mountain air.

When all at once
She heard the familiar sound

Of a minivan door;
Slide open,
Slide shut.

Warm, homely babble,
Voices she had missed.

She leaned over the balcony
And waved to her family
Before rushing down the side steps
To greet them.

That night they all camped
On the tiny, living room floor;
Sleeping bags,
Spare blankets,
Dim lights,
And mugs
Steaming with chocolat chaud.

"Do you think the princess
Will ever return home?"
The youngest asked
Her older brother and sisters.

"Mais bien sûr."
Papa entered the room.
"Don't forget, le pirate and le prince."

Le Prince et le Pirate

No one dared to move,
They hardly breathed.
Would it come back?
Who was next?

The pirates looked to their captain,
The soldiers to their prince.
Would they go after the beast?
Would it be a race to to the peak?

The pirate king moved first;
Grinding his teeth,
Clenching his fist.
He kicked at the sand,
Then returned to his ship.

The prince moved in haste;
He called for his men.
They rushed
To the base of the mountain.

Then a sea horn froze them midstride;
A commotion from the pirates
As they called out to the kingsmen.

The pirate king stood
At the front of his line,
White flag in hand,
Rippling in the wind.

The prince stepped forward.
He listened to
The proud pirate preach
Of the dangers ahead
And the treasure they both sought.

To survive the mountain
Forces must be joined,
Blades shared.
Then at the top
Fate would decide
Which ship would return home.

A prince and a pirate.

Last Story

Papa pushed the last suitcase
Into the small rental car

The sun was setting
Over the mountains
Through the ancient apple orchard.
Puddles of orange rays
Rest on the dirt road.

In front of the house,
In the middle of the woods,
Around the bend.

Older sister shed a tear
Watching from the porch.
She was in anticipation
Of the early morning ahead,
Of the week to come,
But not of the goodbyes.

"Maman made tea!"
Younger sister stepped onto the porch,
Tray in hand.
"Papa, you can't let her leave
Without finishing the story."

The rest of the family
Assembled on the porch.
Brother sat on the railing,
Sisters dragged out chairs.

One last story.

"The prince and the pirate set off to save la
belle."

La Belle

The strange company advanced,
Through forest thick as jungle.
They encountered many evils
Faced fearsome foes.

One by one
Pirates turned away,
For they no longer
Saw any worth in sight.

But the soldiers
Fought on;
Sword in hand,
Sheild at the ready.
They would fight
Until death.

They finally reached
The mountain's peak
And there they found
The dragon's domain.

A cavernous dwelling,
Large as the king's castle,
Darker than a night
Without the moon or stars

Inside the princess sat,
Besides the sleeping beast.
She had soothed him with her voice,
Had quieted him with her song.

One by one she chipped away
At his armored scales.

But the arrival of men
Shook the dragon awake
The moment he caught
A trail of their scent.

Wrathfully he stood,
Unfurling his wings,
Before soaring out into the open
And arising into the air.

Vexed and provoked,
The dragon let lose
A stream of flame to the forest.
The retreating pirates
Were scorched.

The soldiers however were ready;
Bows strung,
Spears in hand,
The prince at their head.

The pirate king found himself abandoned.

Lances were thrust,
Arrows flew,
And in a moment of valor
The prince climbed a great oak.

There he took his last arrow,
A weapon with a head of gold,
And set his to his bow.

To his astonishment he saw
A small weakness,
A vulnerability.

In a moment outside of time
He aimed his arrow
And like a golden bird it flew
Burying itself into the dragon's heart.

The kingsmen cheered
But the prince would not yet
Celebrate victory

He rushed into the cavern
In search of his princess
And there he found her;

Standing on a ledge
Like a ray of light
Over a dead pirate king
His head crushed by a stone.

Now my dear children,
Listen closely to the end of the tale,
For this part is complete
Yet the story does not end.

The prince married the princess
And when the old king died
They ascended the throne
To rule the kingdom;
Justly,
Courageously,
Valiantly,
Compassionately.

The new king would never cease
To love his beauty
To protect
To serve
Until their adventures came to an end,
When they closed their eyes
To eternal rest.

Now let it be known
The Dragon Story
Is a story of measures;
Measures that must be taken
In order to preserve true beauty.

It is a tale of a prince;
His valor,
His virtue,
And his willingness to
Overcome evil.

For only a fool
Would not travel
To the ends of the earth
To love
To protect
And to serve
The beautiful truth.

www.ingramcontent.com/pod-product-compliance
Lightning Source LLC
Chambersburg PA
CBHW071454150726
48000CB00006B/2559